The Way

A Catholic Small Group Discussion Guide

The Evangelical Catholic
Follow Jesus Series

www.evangelicalcatholic.org

Table of Contents

Introduction

"Come, follow me." Matthew 4:19

Jesus spoke these simple words to his disciples long ago. Jesus speaks the same words to us today. We can hear it in the restlessness of our hearts amidst the frantic pace of modern life. We can sense it in our most honest yearnings for purpose in a world inundated with distraction. This introductory small group guide is designed to beckon wih this same call, "Come, follow me." All of us are called to pursue "the way, the truth, and the life"(Jn 14:6) that is not a *something*, but a *someone*: the Word made flesh, God incarnated in the person of Jesus Christ.

In his first encyclical letter, *Deus Caritas Est* (God is Love), our Holy Father Benedict XVI reminds us: "Being Christian is not the result of an ethical choice, or a lofty idea, but the encounter with an event, a person." This person is of course Jesus Christ, the cornerstone of our faith and the reason for our hope. Pope John Paul II proclaimed Christ as "the foundation and center of history, its meaning and ultimate goal" (*Novo Millennio Ineunte, 5*). This person — Jesus Christ, the center and ultimate goal of human history — is the foundation and focal point for all studies in the Follow Jesus series.

> *"Christ is the foundation and center of history; He is its meaning and ultimate goal."*
>
> **Pope John Paul II**
> ***Novo Millennio Ineuente, 5***

Our purpose here is to stimulate an actual encounter with the living God, with Jesus Christ risen from the dead. In communion with the U.S. Conference of Catholic Bishops, we hope that the following reflections will help people "consciously grow in the life of Christ through experience, reflection, prayer and study" (USCCB, *Our Hearts Were*

Burning Within Us). In addition to a presentation of truths regarding Our Lord and his Church, *The Way* seeks to facilitate a deeply personal, yet at the same time communal encounter with God.

We all long for deep friendship with our brothers and sisters in Christ. These types of friendships form when we can gather together to express and solidify that which bonds us for eternity — our faith and hope in God through Jesus Christ. Our common baptism binds the Church together and makes the way for Christian community. It is hoped that for each participant, *The Way* might become an avenue for truly intentional Christian community — one that reflects the manifold gifts of the body of Christ, one that nourishes real growth in each disciple of Jesus, one that responds to the call of Christ to be a light unto the world (Mt 5:13).

John Paul II promoted small Christian communities as a means of evangelization, an instrument for effectively sharing the Good News of Jesus Christ in the world. Being a part of a thriving small group promotes substantial spiritual growth and even conversion, and this sort of holy vitality quite naturally spills over into the lives of others. As Pope John Paul II noted, "Those who have come into genuine contact with Christ cannot keep him for themselves, they must proclaim him" (*Novo Millennio Ineunte*, *40*).

Matter of fact, mature disciples who are continually enlivened by their encounters with Christ are positively brilliant when it comes to sharing the Gospel. There is perhaps no one who is more excited to share the beauty of Jesus than one who has just met him. In the same way we are compelled to impart good news or fortune with those around us, there is nothing more natural after having received the ultimate "good news" (or Gospel) of Jesus Christ than to burst forth and share this great gift with the world. This is the heart of Catholic evangelization.

It is our continually confirmed experience that effective small groups can facilitate deep, personal encounters with God which will bear the fruit of evangelization for years to come. Small groups can help re-awaken the evangelical impulse of our tradition and reposition evangelization as the "center of the Church's mission and her deepest identity" (Pope Paul VI, *Evangelii Nuntiandi*, 14). After a personal and life-changing encounter with Christ, we cannot help but share with others the Good News. *Out of the overflow of the heart, the mouth speaks.* Matthew 12:34

Effective small groups facilitate a deeper and more penetrating experience of the principle means by which we celebrate intimate union with Christ – the liturgy. *The Way* can and should be understood in light of its ultimate connection to the Church's wor-

> "These communities are a sign of vitality within the Church, an instrument of formation and evangelization, and a solid starting point for a new society based on 'civilization of love.'"
>
> **Pope John Paul II,**
> **Mission of the Redeemer, 51**

ship, belief, and activity. By digging into the sacred sources—Scripture and Tradition—we are better able to unearth the profound mystery of Emmanuel—"God-with-us." The engagement in the Christian mystery through small group prayer, study, and discussion, better enables us to embrace and appropriate God's supreme gift to us through the Eucharist, "the source and summit of the Christian life" (*Sacramentum Concilium,* 47).

In this way, *The Way* strengthens the relationship between worship and belief. The same process of reading and prayer that we use in each week's *The Way* group can be used in our personal prayer at home. Time, set aside to focus on God, opens our eyes to realize how amazingly close he is to us in every moment. Christ's presence at Mass comes alive to us. As we learn to see him in our daily lives, we see him better at Mass, especially as we receive him in the Eucharist.

While the celebration of the Eucharistic liturgy is the principal place we encounter God, grow strong in faith, and are equipped for mission in the kingdom of God, a small Christian community is a natural complement and enhancement of these ends. We hope that this introductory small group guide will help you further encounter Jesus Christ, the center and cornerstone of our faith, giving your life "a new horizon and decisive direction." We pray that these studies will inspire you to place Christ at the center of your lives and help you to grow in the likeness of the One we call both friend and savior.

> *"Those who have come into genuine contact with Christ cannot keep him for themselves, they must proclaim him."*
>
> **Pope John Paul II,**
> ***Novo Millennio Ineunte, 40***

All in all, our goal through *The Way* is none other than to help you to discover and rediscover that "God is love, and he who abides in love abides in God, and God abides in him" (1 Jn 4:16). We follow the pastoral principle which frames the whole life of the Church and all her endeavors — "Whether something is proposed for belief, for hope or for action, the love of our Lord must always be made accessible, so that anyone can see that all the works of perfect Christian virtue spring from love and have no other objective than to arrive at love" (*Roman Catechism*, Preface, 10). Our prayer is that your love may "abound more and more" (Phil 1:9) and your witness to Jesus Christ might plant the seeds for a "new springtime of evangelization" (JPII) in the Church and throughout the world. Hear the words of Jesus today, "Come, follow me," and experience the truth that will set you free (Jn 8:32).

"One way of renewing parishes, especially for parishes in large cities, might be to consider the parish as a community of communities.

"It seems timely therefore to form ecclesial communities and groups of a size that allows for true human relationships. This will make it possible to live communion more intensely, ensuring that it is fostered not only ad intra, but also with the parish communities to which such groups belong and with the entire diocesan and universal Church.

"In such a human context it will be easier to gather to hear the word of God, to reflect on the range of human problems in the light of this word and gradually to make responsible decisions inspired by the all-embracing love of Christ."

Pope John Paul II,
The Church in America

Session I: Friendship with Christ

"I no longer call you servants...
Instead I call you friends." John 15:15

Opening Prayer

Invite all participants to pray aloud the following prayer by Saint Anselm of Canterbury (1033 A.D. -1109 A.D).

O Lord, our God, teach our hearts this day where and how to see you, where and how to find you.

You have made us and remade us, and you have bestowed on us all the good things we possess, and still we do not know you.

We have not yet done that for which we were made. Teach us to seek you, for we cannot seek you unless you teach us, or find you unless you show yourself to us. Let us seek you in our desire; let us desire you in our seeking.

Let us find you by loving you; let us love you when we find you. We pray through Jesus Christ, Our Lord.

Amen.

Sharing Our Experience

Take a couple minutes to turn to a partner and tell them about your best friend. Use the following questions as loose guidelines for your conversation.

- What is your best friend like?

- What first attracted you to your best friend?

- How do you spend time together?

- Talk about your conversations — why are they so good/interesting?

- What makes your friendship solid?

- What habits do you need in order to cultivate your friendship?

- How have you changed since you met your friend?

- What could endanger your friendship?

Group discussion to summarize together.

- What stood out to you during your conversation?

- What then are the key elements to a good friendship?

- What are some things that get in the way of good friendship?

- Have you ever considered God to be a friend? Why or why not?

- Compare the key elements of a good friendship to your relationship with God. On a scale of 1-10, how would you assess your "friendship" with God (1 being "don't even know him" and 10 being "best friends")? Explain.

Scripture and Tradition

Please invite a participant to read the following passage aloud.

Reading: No matter where you may be with God, he calls each of us into deeper communion, a closer relationship, and yes, even an intimate friendship with him. Yet many of us find it challenging to think about God as our friend. It somehow feels too familiar, too irreverent or even childish. We are more comfortable with a loftier God, a more cosmic Christ, a God marked more by transcendence than familiarity. Reflecting upon the divinity of Christ, St. Paul wrote to the community of believers in Colossae:

Reading: Colossians 1:15-20

"¹⁵He is the image of the invisible God, the first-born of all creation; ¹⁶for in him all things were created, in heaven and on earth, visible and invisible, whether thrones or dominions or principalities or authorities — all things were created through him and for him. ¹⁷He is before all things, and in him all things hold together. ¹⁸He is the head of the body, the church; he is the beginning, the first-born from the dead, that in everything he might be pre-eminent.

> *"Christ is the foundation and center of history;*
>
> *He is its meaning and ultimate goal."*
>
> **Pope John Paul II,**
> ***Novo Millenio Ineunte, 40***

"¹⁹For in him all the fullness of God was pleased to dwell, ²⁰and through him to reconcile to himself all things, whether on earth or in heaven, making peace by the blood of his cross."

12

- **How do you think about or understand God? Is God more distant for you or is he close? Familiar or removed? Personable or inaccessible? Explain.**

- **What are some of the fears we all share in opening ourselves up to a friendship with Christ?**

Please invite a participant to read the following aloud.

Reading: You might find that Paul's image of Christ in this passage reflects the way you feel about God. This majestic portrait of Jesus Christ is wondrous, awe-inspiring, and absolutely true. Yet it would fall short of revealing the fuller nature of God if it did not also disclose the thoroughly personal, familiar, and human side of the Lord. While most of us are very comfortable with God as Creator, many of us don't know what to do with God who calls us into intimate friendship with him.

Reading: Pope Benedict XVI, Inaugural Homily

"Are we not perhaps all afraid in some way? If we let Christ enter fully into our lives, if we open ourselves totally to him, are we not afraid that He might take something away from us? Are we not perhaps afraid to give up something significant, something unique, something that makes life so beautiful? Do we not then risk ending up diminished and deprived of our freedom?

> *"Do not be afraid! Throw open the doors to Christ!*
>
> **Pope John Paul II,**
> **Inaugural Address, 1978**

"And once again the Pope (John Paul II) said: No! If we let Christ into our lives, we lose nothing, nothing, absolutely nothing of what makes life free, beautiful and great. No! Only in this friendship are the doors of life opened wide. Only in this friendship is the great potential of human existence truly revealed. Only in this friendship do we experience beauty and liberation.

"And so, today, with great strength and great conviction, on the basis of long personal experience of life, I say to you, dear young people: Do not be afraid of Christ! He takes nothing away, and he gives you everything. When we give ourselves to him, we receive a hundredfold in return. Yes, open, open wide the doors to Christ – and you will find true life. Amen."

- **What spoke to you from this passage?**

- **What challenged you from this passage?**

- **What fears might you have or have you had about an intimate friendship with Christ? Explain.**

- **What does Pope Benedict XVI say will result if we open ourselves to the Lord?**

Reading: John 15:1-11

"¹I am the true vine, and my Father is the vinedresser.

²Every branch of mine that bears no fruit, he takes away, and every branch that does bear fruit he prunes, that it may bear more fruit. ³You are already made clean by the word which I have spoken to you. ⁴Abide in me, and I in you. As the branch cannot bear fruit by itself, unless it abides in the vine, neither can you, unless you abide in me. ⁵I am the vine, you are the branches. He who abides in me, and I in him, he it is that bears much fruit, for apart from me you can do nothing. ⁶If a man does not abide in me, he is cast forth as a branch and withers; and the branches are gathered, thrown into the fire and burned.

⁷"If you abide in me, and my words abide in you, ask whatever you will,

> *"I consider everything a loss compared to the surpassing greatness of knowing Christ Jesus my Lord. . .*
>
> *I consider them rubbish, that I may gain Christ and be found in him. . ."*
>
> **Philippians 3:8**

and it shall be done for you. [8]By this my Father is glorified, that you bear much fruit, and so prove to be my disciples. [9]As the Father has loved me, so have I loved you; abide in my love. [10]If you keep my commandments, you will abide in my love, just as I have kept my Father's commandments and abide in his love. [11]These things I have spoken to you, that my joy may be in you, and that your joy may be full."

- What is the main message of the passage?

- What are some of the recurring phrases?

- What is the relationship between the vine and the branches? How does this metaphor help us to understand what Jesus is saying to us here?

- So, what does it mean to "abide in" or "remain in" Christ? Does the passage give any practical guidance for ways to remain in Christ? What from your conversation about your closest friend might also apply here?

- In Jn 6:56, Jesus said, "He who eats my flesh and drinks my blood abides in me, and I in him." How does Jesus' teaching in John 6:56 compliment this passage?

- How would you explain pruning from God's (the vinedresser's/gardener's) perspective? How would you explain pruning from your perspective (a branch)?

- What kind of pruning have you experienced in your spiritual life? Describe what it was like to go through the pruning. What was the result?

- Did the pruning and the results of the pruning have an impact on your friendship with Christ?

- Where do you see yourself in this passage? You may want to include elements regarding your connection to the vine of Christ, pruning, and fruitfulness.

Connecting to Christ This Week

St. Augustine understood the human condition as restless until finding eternal peace in God, our Creator. To this restlessness Jesus speaks today – "Come to me, all you who are weary and burdened and I will give you rest" (Mt 11:28). Take some time this week to come to Jesus with your anxieties, your weariness, and your burdens. Call out to the One who knows your need and who longs to bring us fulfillment and eternal joy in him.

Readings for reflection this week

- **Psalm 139**

- **John 14-1-14**

- **Matthew 11:25-30**

- **John 8:28-32**

- **Isaiah 55:1-3; Proverbs 3:5-6**

- **Philippians 4:4-9**

- **Prepare for the Sunday Eucharistic Liturgy by meditating on the Scripture readings from Mass.**

To find the readings go to www.usccb.org/nab/.

Closing Reflection & Prayer

The following is a reflection by the Missionaries of Charity Fathers written as God speaking to us. Please invite a participant to read it aloud. Then take time for any spontaneous prayers of petition, praise, and thanksgiving.

I Thirst for You

It is true. I stand at the door of your heart, day and night. Even when you are not listening, even when you doubt it could be me, I am there. I await even the smallest sign of your response, even the least whispered invitation that will allow Me to enter. And I want you to know that whenever you do invite me, I do come – always and without fail. Silent and unseen I come, but with infinite power and love, and bringing the many gifts of My Spirit. I come with My mercy, with My desire to forgive and heal you, and with a love for you beyond your comprehension – a love every bit as great as the love I have received from the Father. I come, longing to console you and give you my strength, to lift you up and bind all your wounds...Come to Me with your troubles and needs, and with all your longing to be loved... Open to me, for I thirst for you.

Session 2: Prayer

"Come to me, all who labor and are heavy laden, and I will give you rest." Matthew 11:28

Opening Prayer

Invite a participant to read the following prayer (St. Augustine, The Confessions, I, I.) Then open the group in prayer.

Great are you, O Lord, and exceedingly worthy of praise, your power is immense, and your wisdom beyond reckoning. And so we humans, who are a due part of your creation, long to praise you – we who carry our mortality about with us, carry the evidence of our sin and with it the proof that you thwart the proud. Yet these humans, due part of your creation as they are, still do long to praise you. You arouse us so that praising you may bring us joy, because you have made us and drawn us to yourself, and our heart is unquiet until it rests in you.

Please invite a participant to read the following introductory paragraph.

Reading: St. Augustine, in perhaps his most praised work, *The Confessions*, remarked, "You have made us for Yourself, and our heart is restless until it rests in You." In today's fast-paced world it is not difficult to relate to such a statement. It has been said that ours is the age of restlessness. Long hours, heightened pressures, never-ending task lists, and overwhelming demands have many of us running ragged and pulled in a thousand directions. Even when we do settle in at home, instant access to email, voicemail, text messages, and the Internet leave us as harried and distracted at home as we often are at work. It seems that all of our lives, no matter how hard we try to simplify, are characterized by restlessness.

Sharing Our Experience

- **What kinds of things make you restless or anxious?**

- **What do you do to relieve stress in your life? To what extent do those things make you less stressed?**

- **What prevents you from being able to be still, rest, and reflect on your life?**

Please invite a participant to read the following aloud.

Socrates once quipped, "An unexamined life is not worth living." Observing the nature of humanity an Indian holy man noted, "Mind racing – madman; mind quiet – saint; mind still – God." From the divine revelation of sacred Scripture, the Psalmist puts it this way, "Be still and know that I am God" (Ps 46:11). To stop, to quiet ourselves, to reflect on our lives and the One who created us is one of the first steps of knowing the all-knowing, all-present, all-powerful reality of God. This is one way that we might begin to think about a foundational aspect of the Christian life – prayer.

- **How would you define prayer?**

Please invite three participants to read the following passages.

"Prayer is the place of refuge for every worry, a foundation for cheerfulness, a source of constant happiness, a protection against sadness." (St. John Chrysostom)

"For me, prayer is a surge of the heart;

it is a simple look turned toward heaven,
it is a cry of recognition and of love,
embracing both trial and joy."
(St. Thérèse of Lisieux)

"Prayer in my opinion is nothing else than a close sharing between friends;
it means taking time frequently to be alone with him who we know loves us."
(St. Teresa of Avila)

- **Do you relate to any of these definitions of prayer? Explain.**

- **How do you pray? What are some of the ways you speak or abide with Christ?**

Scripture and Tradition

Reading: Luke 11:1-13

[1]He was praying in a certain place, and when he ceased, one of his disciples said to him, 'Lord, teach us to pray, as John taught his disciples.'

[2]And he said to them, 'When you pray, say:

'Father, hallowed be thy name. Thy kingdom come.

[3]Give us each day our daily bread;

[4]and forgive us our sins, for we ourselves forgive every one who is indebted to us;

and lead us not into temptation.'

[5]And he said to them, 'Which of you who has a friend will go to him at midnight and say to him, "Friend, lend me three loaves; [6]for a friend of mine has arrived on a journey, and I have nothing to set before him;" [7]and he will answer from within, "Do not bother me; the door is now shut, and my children are with me in bed; I cannot get up and give you anything?" [8]I tell you, though he will not get up and give him anything because he is his friend, yet because of his importunity he will rise and give him whatever he needs.

[9]And I tell you, Ask, and it will be given you; seek, and you will find; knock, and it will be opened to you.

[10]For every one who asks receives, and he who seeks finds, and to him who knocks it will be opened. [11]What father among you, if his son asks for a fish, will instead of a fish give him a serpent; [12]or if he asks for an egg, will give him a scorpion?

[13]If you then, who are evil, know how to give good gifts to your children, how much more will the heavenly Father give the Holy Spirit to those who ask him!

- If you had to break down the parts of the Our Father into different types of prayer, how would you do so (e.g., petition, praise, thanksgiving, confession, etc.)

- What part(s) is most meaningful to you? How?

- For a 1st century Palestinian Jew, what might have been the significance of calling God "Father"?

- What analogy does the passage give to help us realize the perfect, heavenly Father that we pray to?

- Has parenting or mentoring children been revelatory for you of God's heart for his children (us)? If so, how? How might that apply to conversing with God, petitioning God, and receiving from God?

- When you reflect on the way you pray, are there other aspects of prayer that might broaden your prayer? (ACTS – adoration, confession, thanksgiving, supplication, or petition)

Reading: "Our Father Who Art in Heaven," Pope Benedict XVI *Jesus of Nazareth*, 135-137

"'The Our Father begins with a great consolation: we are allowed to say 'Father.' This one word contains the whole history of redemption. We are allowed to say 'Father' because the Son was our brother and has revealed the Father to us; because, thanks to what Christ has done, we have once more become children of God. . . We must therefore let Jesus teach us what father really means. . . The love that endures 'to the end' (Jn 13:1), which the Lord fulfilled on the Cross in praying for his enemies, shows us the essence of the Father.

> ""The gift of God is God himself."
>
> **Pope Benedict XVI**

"Let us consider a further text as well. The Lord reminds us that fathers do not give their children stones when they ask for bread. He then goes on to say: 'If you then, who are evil, know how to give good gifts to your children, how much more will your Father who is in heaven give good things to those who ask him!' (Mt. 7:9). Luke specifies the 'good gifts' that the Father gives; he says 'how much more will the heavenly Father give the Holy Spirit to those who ask him!'

"This means that the gift of God is God himself. The 'good things' that he gives us are himself. This reveals in a surprising way what prayer is really all about: It is not about this or that, but about God's desire to offer us the gift of himself – that is the gift of all gifts, the 'one thing necessary.' Prayer is a way of gradually purifying and correcting our wishes and of slowly coming to realize what we really need: God and his Spirit."

- According to the passage, what is the gift of God?

- How does this view of what happens in prayer and what we receive in prayer impact your understanding of prayer?

- Where and when do you pray? What is your style of prayer? Do you speak aloud or sit quietly? What has worked for you?

- **What are some practical things that have helped you to regularly set aside time for prayer?**

Connecting to Christ This Week

It is crucial to find time in your life to pray everyday. Identify a time when you can get up, "long before dawn," and find a solitary place to pray. Make prayer a first priority in your day. Open your ears that you may truly hear God's eternal Word, Jesus Christ our Lord. Commit to a certain duration for prayer and guard it in your schedule as you would guard a date with a special friend.

If possible, try to attend daily Mass and/or go to the Sacrament of Reconciliation this week. At Mass, Jesus makes clear his desire for friendship and connection with us through the Scripture readings and by giving his life to us in the Eucharist. Confession gives us a chance to heal our friendship with Christ if we know that we have done things to hinder it.

> *"Morning after morning he opens my ear that I may hear."*
>
> **Isaiah 50:4**

Find a friend (perhaps from the group, but not necessarily) to help you with your commitment to prayer. We often call these friends "accountability partners." Ask your accountability partner to meet with you (or speak to you over the phone) once a week to discuss your experience of prayer and spiritual growth. The following questions/steps can serve as a simple guide for your time together:

- **Did you follow your plan for the week concerning Scripture reading and prayer?**

- **Was there anything from your reading and prayer that was particularly meaningful for you this week? Did you have any questions?**

Were you blessed with any inspirations or insights?

- What were some challenges and/or victories from prayer this week?

- What do you need prayer for in the coming week? Share and discuss.

- Pray together about the upcoming week.

Readings for reflection this week

- Psalm 139

- Jeremiah 29:12-14

- Ephesians 6: 10-20

- Philippians 4:6-7

- Matthew 6:1-8

- Psalm 27

Closing Reflection & Prayer

Please invite a participant to read the following prayer/reflection. Invite participants to add their own prayers following this prayer/reflection. Invite someone to close the group in prayer at the appropriate time.

Almighty God and Father,
Over this last week I have tried to understand your love for me and the entire people of God you created for your glory. I don't claim to fully understand your love, but I am trying to open myself to you and the love you have planned for me from the beginning.
I know that you have loved me and blessed me in ways I could not have imagined.

So please, dear Father, help me to remember your great –love — when I wonder about my worthiness, when I fall into doubt, when I am inclined to be unloving. I want your love to be reflected in my daily life. Thank you for loving us in a way we can understand. And thank you for loving us first. Amen. [1]

---

[1] Is it better to pray by reading a formal prayer of the Church, perhaps drawn from the rich history of our tradition? Or is it more pleasing to God that we pray with our own words, or as many put it, that we "pray from the heart"? Of course, both methods are wonderful ways to express our faith, hope, and love of the One who made us, who lived for us, who died and rose again for us. Some Christians, however, may only be comfortable with reciting a prayer written by another, typically a noted saint or icon of the faith. Spontaneous prayer may seem too personal, vulnerable, or even intimidating. Though both types of prayer are good, necessary, and encouraged by the Church, many blessings accrue from praying spontaneously, using not another's words but your own. Sometimes our own "words" or expressions of prayer might be loving, attentive silence.

Peter Kreeft, noted author and professor of philosophy at Boston College, commented: "When we use the prayers of the Church, we use the greatest prayers ever written, the words and sentiments of great saints and hymn writers and liturgists. We do this rightly, because God deserves the best, and these prayers are the best. They were composed by other people, but we make them our own when we pray them, like a lover reciting a sonnet by Shakespeare to his beloved. . .But if others' words are the only words lovers use to each other, they are not lovers but performers. We must not only 'say our prayers', we must pray. Others' words may be more beautiful, but your words are more yours, and God cherishes them as a father cherishes his child's own crude drawing made just for him more than he cherishes the greatest work of art in the world. God wants your own words most of all because they are your own; they come from your heart, and your heart is what your Lover craves" (Kreeft, Prayer for Beginners, 29-30).

Session 3: Sacred Scripture

"For the word of God is living and active, sharper than any two-edged sword, piercing to the division of soul and spirit, of joints and marrow, and discerning the thoughts and intentions of the heart." Hebrews 4:12

Please invite all participants to pray together this prayer by Origen (ca. 185-254).

Opening Prayer

Lord, inspire us to read your Scriptures and to meditate upon them day and night. We beg you to give us real understanding of what we need, that we in turn may put its precepts into practice. Yet we know that understanding and good intentions are worthless, unless rooted in your graceful love. So we ask that the words of Scriptures may also be not just signs on a page, but channels of grace into our hearts.

We pray this through Jesus Christ, our Lord. Amen.

Sharing Our Experience

In the last session, we discussed how prayer is a well-spring of grace, a central and essential means to communion or friendship with Christ. Today's reflection on Sacred Scripture is related to personal prayer. As the Dogmatic Constitution on Divine Revelation, 25 (*Dei Verbum*) from Vatican II states:

> "Prayer should accompany the reading of sacred scripture, so that it becomes a dialogue between God and the human reader. For, as St. Ambrose said, 'we speak to him when we pray; we listen to him when we read the divine oracles.'"

Each one of us comes to this group with different conceptions of and experiences with Scripture.

- **What has been your experience of Scripture?**

- **What comes to mind for you when you hear the word "Bible"?**

Scripture and Tradition

Please invite a participant to read the following paragraph aloud.

Reading: Document from Vatican Council II — *Dei Verbum (The Dogmatic Constitution on Divine Revelation)*, paragraph 21

The Church has always venerated the divine scriptures as it has venerated the Body of the Lord, in that it never ceases, above all in the sacred liturgy, to partake of the bread of life and to offer it to the faithful from the one table of the word of God and the Body of Christ. It has always regarded and continues to regard the scriptures, taken together with sacred tradition, as the supreme rule of its faith. For, since they are inspired by God and committed to writing once and for all time, they present God's own word in unalterable form, and they make the voice of the Holy Spirit sound again and again in the words of the prophets and apostles. It follows that all the preaching of the church, as indeed the entire Christian religion, should be nourished and ruled by sacred scripture. In the sacred books the Father who is in heaven comes lovingly to meet his children, and talks with them. And such is the force and power of the word of God that it is the church's support and strength, imparting robustness to the faith of its daughters and sons and providing food for their souls. It is a pure and unfailing fount of spiritual life. It is eminently true of Holy Scripture that: 'The word of God is living and active' (Heb 4:12), and 'is able to build you up and to give you the inheritance among all those who are sanctified' (Acts 20:32; see 1 Th 2:13).[2]

> "In the sacred books, the Father who is in heaven comes lovingly to meet his children and talks to them."
>
> **Dei Verbum, 21**

- What stands out to you in this paragraph?

- What are some of the ways the Church describes and defines Sacred Scripture and Sacred Tradition? What are some of the statements that describe how the Church regards Sacred Scripture?

- How do you explain that the Father "comes lovingly to meet his children, and talks with them," when they read Scripture?

- How does the Church describe the impact that Scripture can have on one's relationship to Christ?

- Have you experienced Scripture as God coming lovingly to meet you and talk with you? If yes, how did that affect your relationship with Christ?

- What from this document challenges you? How?

---

[2]Austin Flannery, O.P., *The Basic Sixteen Documents Vatican Council II, Constitutions, Decrees, Declarations.* Northport, New York: Costello) 111-112.

The following reading explores different reactions that people have to the word of God. Please invite two participants to read the following sections aloud.

Reading: Mark 4:1-9, 13-20

¹Again he began to teach beside the sea. And a very large crowd gathered about him, so that he got into a boat and sat in it on the sea; and the whole crowd was beside the sea on the land. ²And he taught them many things in parables, and in his teaching he said to them: ³'Listen! A sower went out to sow. ⁴And as he sowed, some seed fell along the path, and the birds came and devoured it. ⁵Other seed fell on rocky ground, where it had not much soil, and immediately it sprang up, since it had no depth of soil; ⁶and when the sun rose it was scorched, and since it had no root it withered away. ⁷Other seed fell among thorns and the thorns grew up and choked it, and it yielded no grain. ⁸And other seeds fell into good soil and brought forth grain, growing up and increasing and yielding thirtyfold and sixtyfold and a hundredfold.' ⁹And he said, 'He who has ears to hear, let him hear.'

> "It must be said that Sacred Scripture is divinely ordered to this: that through it, the truth necessary for salvation may be made known to us."
>
> **St. Thomas Aquinas**

¹³And he said to them, 'Do you not understand this parable? How then will you understand all the parables? ¹⁴The sower sows the word. ¹⁵And these are the ones along the path, where the word is sown; when they hear, Satan immediately comes and takes away the word which is sown in them. ¹⁶And these in like manner are the ones sown upon rocky ground, who, when they hear the word, immediately receive it with joy; ¹⁷and they have no root in themselves, but endure for a while; then, when tribulation or persecution arises on account of the word, immediately they fall away. ¹⁸And others are the ones sown among thorns; they are those who hear the word, ¹⁹but the cares of the world,

and the delight in riches, and the desire for other things, enter in and choke the word, and it proves unfruitful. [20]But those that were sown upon the good soil are the ones who hear the word and accept it and bear fruit, thirtyfold and sixtyfold and a hundredfold.'

- **What does Jesus say the seed represents? (see v. 4:14) What do the types of soil represent?**

- **Describe the different human responses to the word of God that each type of soil represents.**

- **Jesus likens rocky ground to the person who has no root in themselves. They receive the word with joy and endure for a while but when tribulation comes on account of the word, they fall away. What are some contemporary examples of tribulation that could come on account of the word?**

- **What might be some modern-day examples of thorns?**

- **How can thorns choke out the word of God in a person's heart?**

- **Take a couple minutes in silence to reflect on and even write down which type(s) of soil you most identify with and why. Then come together as a group and share.**

- **Please invite a participant to read the following section aloud.**

In all relationships, communication is essential to growth and intimacy. Our relationship with Christ is no different. The more we listen to God as we read Scripture, the more we get to know Jesus Christ and hear the Holy Spirit speak to us personally in our daily lives. St. Jerome went so far as to say "ignorance of the scriptures is ignorance of Christ." In addition, the Church "forcefully and specifically exhorts all the Christian faithful...to learn 'the surpassing knowledge of Jesus Christ' (Phil 3:8) by frequent reading of the divine scriptures."[3] The Church also teaches that "prayer should accompany the reading of sacred scripture, so that it becomes a dialogue between God and the

> *"The Word of God is in your heart. The Word digs in this soil so that the spring may gush out."*
>
> **Origen (ca. 185-254)**

---

[3]Austin Flannery, O.P., *The Basic Sixteen Documents Vatican Council II*, 114.

human reader".

- **What are some practical ways to integrate Scripture into daily life and prayer?**

Connecting to Christ This Week

Set aside a place and time each day when you can read Scripture, reflect, and pray.

Readings for reflection this week

- **Luke 12: 13-34**

- **Romans 5: 1-10**

- **1 Peter 5: 1-11**

- **Colossians 3: 1-17**

- **Mark 10: 17-31**

- **2 Corinthians 4:16 - 2 Corinthians 5:10**

- **In preparation for Sunday's liturgy, read and pray about the readings. To find the readings go to www.usccb.org/nab/ and click on the upcoming Sunday.**

> *"All Sacred Scripture is but one book, and that one book is Christ."*
>
> **Hugh of St. Victor (ca. 1078-1141)**

Closing Reflection & Prayer

After someone opens the group in prayer, take time for spontaneous prayers of petition, thanksgiving, and praise. Then pray the following Psalm (Ps 119:89-105) by reading it together as a closing prayer.

For ever, O Lord, thy word is firmly fixed in the heavens.
Thy faithfulness endures to all generations;
thou hast established the earth, and it stands fast.
By thy appointment they stand this day;
for all things are thy servants.
If thy law had not been my delight,
I should have perished in my affliction.
I will never forget thy precepts;
for by them thou hast given me life.
I am thine, save me; for I have sought thy precepts.
The wicked lie in wait to destroy me;
but I consider thy testimonies.
I have seen a limit to all perfection,
but thy commandment is exceedingly broad.
Oh, how I love thy law! It is my meditation all the day.
Thy commandment makes me wiser than my enemies,
for it is ever with me.
I have more understanding than all my teachers,
for thy testimonies are my meditation.
I understand more than the aged, for I keep thy precepts.
I hold back my feet from every evil way,

in order to keep thy word.
I do not turn aside from thy ordinances, for thou hast
taught me.
How sweet are thy words to my taste,
sweeter than honey to my mouth!
Through thy precepts I get understanding;
therefore I hate every false way.

Thy word is a lamp to my feet
and a light to my path.
We pray this through Jesus Christ, our Lord.
Amen.

Session 4: The Eucharist: Intimate Friendship with Christ

"The Eucharist, as a mystery to be 'lived', meets each of us as we are, and makes our concrete existence the place where we experience daily the radical newness of the Christian life."

Pope Benedict XVI, Sacramentum Caritatis

Opening Prayer

Open by reading the following prayer of St. Thomas Aquinas (ca. 1225-1274).

Grant me, O Lord my God,
a mind to know you,
a heart to seek you,
wisdom to find you,
conduct pleasing to you,
faithful perseverance in waiting for you,
and a hope of finally embracing you.
Amen.

"I Call You Friends" John 15:15

Our first session began with this call of Our Lord to intimate friendship with him. In this session we explore the context in which Jesus stated these words and accomplished this most profound intimacy with us — in his institution of the Eucharist at the Last Supper.

- **What has been your experience of Mass?**

Sharing Our Experience

- Which part(s) of Mass do you connect with most easily? What parts are more challenging for you?

Scripture and Tradition

Please invite two or three participants to read the following section aloud.

The reading that follows is part of the Bread of Life discourse in the Gospel of John. What precedes this section of John 6 is the miracle of the feeding of the five thousand, the only miracle recorded in each of the four Gospels. Then Jesus walks on the sea towards his disciples who are in a boat. They are terrified of him but Jesus says to them, "It is I; do not be afraid" (6:20). The next day, having been fed by Jesus through the multiplication of the loaves, the crowd goes looking for Jesus.

Reading: John 6: 25-40, 51-58

[25]When they found him on the other side of the sea, they said to him, 'Rabbi, when did you come here?' [26]Jesus answered them, 'Truly, truly, I say to you, you seek me, not because you saw signs, but because you ate your fill of the loaves. [27]Do not labor for the food which perishes, but for the food which endures to eternal life, which the Son of man will give to you; for on him has God the Father set his seal.' [28]Then they said to him, 'What must we do, to be doing the works of God?' [29]Jesus answered them, 'This is the work of God, that you believe in him

whom he has sent.' [30]So they said to him, 'Then what sign do you do, that we may see, and believe you? What work do you perform? [31]Our fathers ate the manna in the wilderness; as it is written, "He gave them bread from heaven to eat."' [32]Jesus then said to them, 'Truly, truly, I say to you, it was not Moses who gave you the bread from heaven; my Father gives you the true bread from heaven. [33]For the bread of God is that which comes down from heaven, and gives life to the world.' [34]They said to him, 'Lord, give us this bread always.'

> "Lord Jesus, Who in the Eucharist make your dwelling among us and become our traveling companion, sustain our Christian communities so that they may be ever more open to listening and accepting your Word."
>
> **Pope John Paul II**

[35]Jesus said to them, 'I am the bread of life; he who comes to me shall not hunger, and he who believes in me shall never thirst. [36]But I said to you that you have seen me and yet do not believe. [37]All that the Father gives me will come to me; and him who comes to me I will not cast out. [38]For I have come down from heaven, not to do my own will, but the will of him who sent me; [39]and this is the will of him who sent me, that I should lose nothing of all that he has given me, but raise it up at the last day. [40]For this is the will of my Father, that every one who sees the Son and believes in him should have eternal life; and I will raise him up at the last day.'"

'[51]I am the living bread which came down from heaven; if any one eats of this bread, he will live for ever; and the bread which I shall give for the life of the world is my flesh.' [52]The Jews then disputed among themselves, saying, 'How can this man give us his flesh to eat?'

[53]So Jesus said to them, 'Truly, truly, I say to you, unless you eat the flesh of the Son of man and drink his blood, you have no life in you; [54]he who eats my flesh and drinks my blood has eternal life, and I will raise him up at the last day. [55]For my flesh is food indeed, and my blood is drink indeed. [56]He who eats my flesh and drinks my blood abides in

me, and I in him. [57]As the living Father sent me, and I live because of the Father, so he who eats me will live because of me. [58]This is the bread which came down from heaven, not such as the fathers ate and died; he who eats this bread will live for ever.'

> *"I am the living bread which came down from heaven."*
>
> **John 6:51**

- What stood out to you from this passage?

- Describe the progression of the dialogue between Jesus and the crowd. What are they asking and seeking? How does Jesus answer and what is the progression of his words to the crowd?

- What does it mean to labor for food which perishes (v.27)?

- In v. 29 Jesus said, "This is the work of God, that you believe in him whom he has sent." What do you think Jesus means by "believe" here given the context of the preceding miracles and the subsequent verses?

- Have you experienced Jesus as the bread of life, the one who satiates your hunger and quenches your thirst (v. 35)? If so, how?

- What verse(s) most explains the Catholic teaching on the real presence of Christ in the Eucharist? What does eating Christ's flesh and drinking his blood affect in our relationship with God (see vv. 51-56)? Does this resonate with your experience? If so, how? If not, how?

- Where do you see yourself in this passage and why?

Please invite a participant to read the following sections aloud from the *Catechism of the Catholic Church*.

1360 The Eucharist is a sacrifice of thanksgiving to the Father, a blessing by which the Church expresses her gratitude to God for all his benefits, for all that he has accomplished through creation, redemption, and sanctification. Eucharist means first of all "thanksgiving."

1361 The Eucharist is also the sacrifice of praise by which the Church sings the glory of God in the name of all creation. This sacrifice of praise is possible only through Christ: he unites the faithful to his person, to his praise, and to his intercession, so that the sacrifice of praise to the Father is offered through Christ and with him, to be accepted in him.

- **What are some of the Mass parts in which praise and thanksgiving are offered to God?**

- **In which of these Mass parts do you most easily participate fully, actively, and consciously, as the Church calls the People of God to do? Which parts of the Mass are more challenging for you to enter into? Why is that?**

- **What has helped you enter more fully into Mass? What might help you participate even more fully?**

- **Recalling that Eucharist means first of all "thanksgiving," what do you think it would mean to live a 'Eucharistic' life?**

Please invite a participant to read the following excerpts from the _Catechism_ aloud.

1391 Holy Communion augments our union with Christ. The principal fruit of receiving the Eucharist in Holy Communion is an intimate union with Christ Jesus. Indeed, the Lord said: "He who eats my flesh and drinks my blood abides in me, and I in him."

1392 What material food produces in our bodily life, Holy Communion wonderfully achieves in our spiritual life…

> "God dwells in our midst, in the Blessed Sacrament of the altar."
>
> **St. Maximilian Kolbe**

1393 Holy Communion separates us from sin...

1394 As bodily nourishment restores lost strength, so the Eucharist strengthens our charity, which tends to be weakened in daily life; and this living charity wipes away venial sins. By giving himself to us Christ revives our love and enables us to break our disordered attachments to creatures and root ourselves in him…

- **The Catechism also lists and expands on other fruits of Holy Com-**

munion such as the unity of the Mystical Body of Christ, greater commitment to the poor, and the unity of all Christians. Share the fruits (from those listed above or others) that you have experienced through Holy Communion.

- What can we do outside of Mass to be better prepared to experience celebration of the Eucharist as union with Christ? What habits or practices help you experience the Eucharist in a more profound way?

Connecting to Christ This Week

If you don't already attend daily Mass, try to get to a weekday Mass once this week.

Spend some time with Jesus in the Blessed Sacrament at your parish. Reflect on the things that struck you

> *"Do you realize that Jesus is there in the tabernacle expressly for you – for you alone? He burns with the desire to come into your heart."*
>
> **St. Thérèse of Lisieux**

in John 6 or reflect on these rich paragraphs from the *Catechism* listed at the end of this session. Spend time contemplating the mystery of the real presence of Christ in the Eucharist.

Get to Mass early to prepare your heart and mind to receive the Eucharist. Spend a few minutes in thanksgiving to God after Mass. Bring St. Thomas' prayer (below) to pray after receiving the Eucharist.

Readings for personal reflection this week:

- CCC 1374
- CCC 1375
- CCC 1380

- CCC 1381

- In preparation for Sunday's liturgy, read and pray about the readings. To find the readings go to www.usccb.org/nab/ and click on the upcoming Sunday.

Closing Reflection & Prayer

(Prayer after Mass by St. Thomas Aquinas)

If there is time, invite participants to offer spontaneous prayers. Close the session with a corporate recitation of the following prayer.

Lord, Father all-powerful and ever-living God, I thank You, for even though I am a sinner, your unprofitable servant, not because of my worth but in the kindness of your mercy, You have fed me with the Precious Body and Blood of Your Son, our Lord Jesus Christ.

I pray that [this] Holy Communion may not bring me condemnation and punishment but forgiveness and salvation. May it be a helmet of faith and a shield of good will. May it purify me from evil ways and put an end to my evil passions. May it bring me charity and patience, humility and obedience, and growth in the power to do good.

May it be my strong defense against all my enemies, visible and invisible, and the perfect calming of all my evil impulses, bodily and spiritual.

May it unite me more closely to you, the One true God, and lead me safely through death to everlasting happiness with You. And I pray that You will lead me, a sinner, to the banquet where you, with Your Son and holy Spirit, are true and perfect light, total fulfillment, everlasting joy, gladness without end, and perfect happiness to your saints. Grant this through Christ our Lord, Amen.

Session 5: Christian Community

"For where two or three are gathered in my name, there I am in the midst of them." Matthew 18:20

Please invite two participants to read the following paragraphs aloud.

In the beginning the Lord God said, "It is not good for man to be alone"(Gn 2:18). We were never intended to be alone. From the dawn of creation, we were destined to live together in rich community. Bound by deep ties of love, solidarity and self-giving, we were called to live together as one holy people, a united family, the People of God. Pope John Paul II was fond of referring to this body as a "civilization of love," a place governed not by force, power, and greed but by divine charity in light of the Gospel.

This communal vision for the Church is ultimately grounded in the central mystery of the Christian faith – one God in three persons – the Trinity. Although the full mystery of the Trinity eludes our human understanding, the nature of one God revealed in Father, Son, and Holy Spirit sheds light on how we — made in the "image and likeness" of God — are to live in community with one another. Out of the overflow of the triune Godhead, the human family is brought into communion as the People of God. The Father invites all of us, in the life of Jesus Christ, through the action of the Holy Spirit, to share in the divine life and to participate in the very essence of God. In other words, the fundamental nature of God invites us into the deepest and truest sense of community.

This fifth session of the *The Way* series seeks to explore this deeper vision of communion and help us to form, shape, and experience Christian community as a sign of God's presence within and among us.

Opening Prayer

Jesus Christ, our Lord and our brother, you have called us into the very life of God.
You have invited us into your holy presence
and welcomed us into your blessed family, your Church.
Heavenly Father, make us one in faith and hope, and unite us in our commitment to serve your kingdom in love and servanthood.
In our worship and through our daily lives, may the love that binds you in the holy Trinity come to life in our community here. Lord Jesus, send your Spirit to make us one as you and the Father are one. We ask this, Jesus, for you are our Lord and our Savior for ever. Amen.

Sharing Our Experience

- Share the most life-giving experience in community you have known. What made it so special? How did it affect and/or change you?

- If you were moving to a new city, what kind of community would you hope to find in your church? Describe what that community might look like.

Scripture and Tradition

Please invite a participant to read the following passage.

Reading: Acts 2:42-47

⁴²And they devoted themselves to the apostles' teaching and fellowship, to the breaking of bread and the prayers. ⁴³And fear came upon every soul; and many wonders and signs were done through the apostles. ⁴⁴And all who believed were together and had all things in common; ⁴⁵and they sold their possessions and goods and distributed them to all, as any had need.

⁴⁶And day by day, attending the temple together and breaking bread in their homes, they partook of food with glad and generous hearts, ⁴⁷praising God and having favor with all the people. And the Lord added to their number day by day those who were being saved.

- As a group, try to name all of the characteristics of the early Church community listed here in this reading. Is there anything that surprised you? Encouraged you? Challenged you? Why?

- How are these elements of Christian community ideally reflected at Sunday Eucharistic Liturgy?

- How does the community of the early Church compare with the community you experience?

- Today, what do you think gets in the way of this type of Christian community? How could we integrate into our lives some of these principles of Christian community?

Please invite a participant to read the following passage aloud.

Reading: Colossians 3:12-17

¹²Put on then, as God's chosen ones, holy and beloved, compassion, kindness, lowliness, meekness, and patience, ¹³forbearing one another and, if one has a complaint against another, forgiving each other; as the Lord has forgiven you, so you also must forgive.

¹⁴And above all these put on love, which binds everything together in perfect harmony. ¹⁵And let the peace of Christ rule in your hearts, to which indeed you were called in the one body. And be thankful.

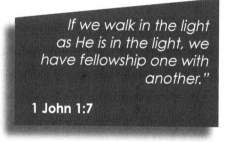

If we walk in the light as He is in the light, we have fellowship one with another."

1 John 1:7

¹⁶Let the word of Christ dwell in you richly, teach and admonish one another in all wisdom, and sing psalms and hymns and spiritual songs with thankfulness in your hearts to God. ¹⁷And whatever you do, in word or deed, do everything in the name of the Lord Jesus, giving thanks to God the Father through him.

- St. Paul uses the image of clothing to describe some key elements of Christian community. What meaning does this image hold for you with regard to these virtues?

- What virtues does St. Paul seem to elevate above the others? Why?

- If God were to speak to you today, what virtue would he ask you to clothe yourself with more often?

- How is living a life clothed with these virtues related to peace in our hearts? As members of the one body of Christ, what does it mean to "let the peace of Christ rule in your hearts"?

- St. Paul talks about forbearance, forgiveness, and teaching and admonishing one another – challenging aspects of close relationships. What has helped you in your struggles to bear with others and forgive others?

- Whether it be with close family members or friends, how might you and I grow in these ways?

Please invite a participant to read the following verse aloud.

Reading: I Thessalonians 2:6b-8

"[6b]Though we might have made demands as apostles of Christ, [7]but we were gentle among you, like a nurse taking care of her children. [8]So, being affectionately desirous of you, we were ready to share with you not only the gospel of God but also our own selves, because you had become very dear to us."

- What is Paul saying in this passage?

- What image does Paul use to describe the care he has for this community? How does this image inform the life of your Christian community?

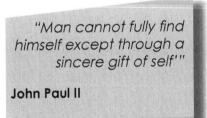

"Man cannot fully find himself except through a sincere gift of self'"

John Paul II

- Why do you think Paul stressed the importance of sharing "not only the gospel of God but also our own selves"? What is the relationship between the Gospel and our lives?

- Share an experience when hearing someone's faith story made a real impact in your life.

- How might taking the time to know another parishioner's faith story make your community more authentic?

Read the following verse aloud.

Reading: Hebrews 10: 23-25

²³Let us hold fast the confession of our hope without wavering, for he who promised is faithful; ²⁴and let us consider how to stir up one another to love and good works, ²⁵not neglecting to meet together, as is the habit of some, but encouraging one another, and all the more as you see the Day drawing near.

- **Why is regular Christian community essential for "holding fast the confession of our hope"(v. 23)?**

- **Many of us have friends and family whom we love dearly who are not practicing Catholic Christians. Though we certainly enjoy some sense of community with them, how can community and friendship with Christians be different?**

Connecting to Christ This Week

- **Do you have authentic Christian friendships that support you in your walk with Christ? If yes, how do those friendships strengthen you? What are some ways to establish those deep connections?**

Reflect on your life in community. Seek the Lord's guidance in how you might better foster a more intimate and authentic community in your church, campus ministry, or group. Go to the Sacrament of Reconciliation this week and seek the Lord's healing presence in the relationships he has given you.

Readings for reflection this week

- John 9:1-34

- Jeremiah 1:4-19

- Acts 22: 3-21

> *"Those who have experienced this know what I am talking about. Those who have not had the experience, well, have the experience and then you will know."*
>
> **St. Bernard of Clairvaux**

- Philippians 3:4-14

- John 4:4-42

- Galatians 1:11-24

Closing Reflection & Prayer

Read the following prayer aloud, each paragraph read by a different participant.

In the name of the Father, and the Son, and the Holy Spirit. Amen.

Lord Jesus, we walk with others who hurt and ache. As we do, keep us closely united to you, Healing Savior, so that our hearts will always be warm with compassion.

We walk with ourselves in our own joys and sorrows. May we look upon our own selves with love, with a belief that we, too, need tending with care.

We walk with our families, communities, loved ones and friends. Our hearts are connected in good times and in bad. May we draw strength from You and be open to the ways in which You call us to be there for each other.

We walk with our world, a world that is filled with pain and grief, with beauty and grandeur. We are all children of the Father. Remind us that who we are and what we do affects our brothers and sisters, the earth, and all creatures.

We walk with wounds yet to be healed. In our communities and in our own lives, do not let us run from what we need to face. Grant us the courage to let go of whatever keeps us

48

from being healed. Help us to trust You with our lives, oh loving God.

We walk with scars that tell of the tough times we have had. Our wounds can be our teachers. God of wisdom, draw us to quiet times of reflection so that we can see and accept the truths that our wounded times have offered us.

We walk in your presence, Triune God. May our inner vision keep us closely bonded with You. Assure us often that we are all a part of the Body of Christ. When we meet one another, we meet You. May the treasure of our union with You energize us and renew us as we reach out to others.

O Divine Father, guide and direct our times of sharing. May we listen attentively to the stories you are telling through our lives and the lives of others, and may we always remember Your presence among us.
In the name of the Father, and the Son, and the Holy Spirit. Amen.[4]

---

[4]Adapted from Charles Garfield, Wisdom Circles, 1998; Thomas A. Kleissler, Small Christian Communities: A Vision of Hope, 1991; Jean Vanier, Becoming Human, 1998.

Session 6: Initial and Ongoing Conversion

"Therefore, if anyone is in Christ, he is a new creation; the old has gone, the new has come!"
2 Corinthians 5:17

Opening Prayer

Please invite a participant to be the "leader."

Leader: Come, Holy Spirit, fill the hearts of your faithful and enkindle in them the fire of your love. Send forth your Spirit and they shall be created.
All: And you shall renew the face of the earth.
All: O God, who by the light of the Holy Spirit, did instruct the hearts of the faithful, grant us in the same Spirit to be truly wise and ever to rejoice in His consolation. Through Christ our Lord, Amen.

Sharing Our Experience

- What do you think of when you hear the word "conversion"? How does the word "conversion" make you feel?

- What would you say "conversion" is?

Scripture and Tradition

Please invite two participants to read the following passage aloud.

Reading: Luke 15: 1-2, 11-32

The parable of the prodigal son is at the end of a string of three parables that all end with celebration and parties. The opening verses of Chapter 15 provide a helpful context:

¹Now the tax collectors and sinners were all drawing near to hear him. ²And the Pharisees and the scribes murmured, saying, 'This man receives sinners and eats with them.' So he told them this parable:

¹¹And he said, 'There was a man who had two sons; ¹²and the younger of them said to his father, "Father, give me the share of property that falls to me." And he divided his living between them. ¹³Not many days later, the younger son gathered all he had and took his journey into a far country, and there he squandered his property in loose living. ¹⁴And when he had spent everything, a great famine arose in that country, and he began to be in want. ¹⁵So he went and joined himself to one of the citizens of that country, who sent him into his fields to feed swine. ¹⁶And he would gladly have fed on the pods that the swine ate; and no one gave him anything. ¹⁷But when he came to himself he said, "How many of my father's hired servants have bread enough and to spare, but I perish here with hunger! ¹⁸I will arise and go to my father, and I will say to him,

> "My son was dead and is alive again; he was lost, and is found."
>
> **Luke 15:24**

'Father, I have sinned against heaven and before you; ¹⁹I am no longer worthy to be called your son; treat me as one of your hired servants.'

[20]And he arose and came to his father. But while he was yet at a distance, his father saw him and had compassion, and ran and embraced him and kissed him. [21]And the son said to him, "Father, I have sinned against heaven and before you; I am no longer worthy to be called your son." [22]But the father said to his servants, "Bring quickly the best robe, and put it on him; and put a ring on his hand, and shoes on his feet; [23]and bring the fatted calf and kill it, and let us eat and make merry; [24]for this my son was dead, and is alive again; he was lost, and is found." And they began to make merry.

'[25]Now his elder son was in the field; and as he came and drew near to the house, he heard music and dancing. [26]And he called one of the servants and asked what this meant. [27]And he said to him, "Your brother has come, and your father has killed the fatted calf, because he has received him safe and sound." [28]But he was angry and refused to go in. His father came out and entreated him, [29]but he answered his father, "Lo, these many years I have served you, and I never disobeyed your command; yet you never gave me a kid, that I might make merry with my friends. [30]But when this son of yours came, who has devoured your living with harlots, you killed for him the fatted calf!" [31]And he said to him, "Son, you are always with me, and all that is mine is yours. [32]It was fitting to make merry and be glad, for this your brother was dead, and is alive; he was lost, and is found."'"

- What are some of the themes of this parable?

- Note all of the father's actions towards both of his sons in the parable (you may want to circle them). What words would you use to describe the father based on his actions?

- Why do you think the prodigal son wanted to leave his father's house? How would you outline his process of conversion? What words would you use to describe the prodigal son based on his actions?

- What was it about Jesus' treatment of sinners and the father's welcoming of the prodigal son that so perturbed the Pharisees and the elder brother? (vv. 22-24)

- What was Jesus trying to reveal about the Father through this simple parable?

- *We all have different images of God the Father, even if we profess the same faith, because of our diverse familial, religious, and personal backgrounds. We might say we believe in God the Father, who is generous and merciful, but our actions towards ourselves, God, and others might reflect otherwise.*

Compare the image of the Father that Jesus conveys to us in Luke 15 and the image that you have of God the Father. How are they different or similar?

Please invite a participant to read the following paragraph.

Though the brothers are at different stages in the process of conversion, they both are in need of conversion. Making use of the parable to illustrate different steps in the process of continuing conversion, one might say that the prodigal son's interest in the gospel began when he had nothing left and he began to hunger (vv. 16-17).

> "The Christian faith is, above all, conversion to Jesus Christ, full and sincere adherence to his person and the decision to walk in his footsteps."
>
> **General Directory of Catechesis, 53**

His initial conversion followed when he took a step of faith and opted to return to his father. His repentance accompanied this return. The elder brother, on the other hand, had always remained in his father's house. Though faithful to his father, he fell short when he failed to rejoice in his brother's return and spoke bitterly about his father's generosity towards him. The elder brother is in need of the second conversion, the endless task of the whole Church (ongoing conversion).

- **With which brother do you most identify with in this passage? Why?**

Please invite a participant to read the following paragraph aloud.

Reading: *Go and Make Disciples: A National Plan and Strategy for Catholic Evangelization in the United States*, written by the United States Conference of Catholic Bishops in 2002

12. Conversion is the change of our lives that comes about through the power of the Holy Spirit. All who accept the Gospel undergo change as we continually put on the mind of Christ by rejecting sin and becoming more faithful disciples in his Church. Unless we undergo conversion, we have not truly accepted the Gospel.

13. We know that people experience conversion in many ways. Some experience a sudden, shattering insight that brings rapid transformation. Some experience a gradual growth over many years. Others undergo conversion as they take part in the Rite of Christian Initiation of Adults — the normal way adults become members of the Church today. Many experience conversion through the ordinary relationships of family and friends. Others have experienced it through the formation received from Catholic schools and religious education programs. Still others have experienced ongoing conversion in renewals, ecumenical encounters, retreats, parish missions, or through some of the great spiritual movements that have blessed church life today.

> "Lord, I am not worthy to receive you, but only say the word and I shall be healed."

14. This is crucial: we must be converted — and we must continue to be converted! We must let the Holy Spirit change our lives! We must respond to Jesus Christ. And we must be open to the transforming power of the Holy Spirit who will continue to convert us as we follow Christ. If our faith is alive, it will be aroused again and again as we mature as disciples.

15. We can only share what we have received; we can hold on to our faith only if it continues to grow. 'But if salt loses its taste,' Jesus asked, 'with what can it be seasoned?'

- **What from this document strikes you?**

- **How have you experienced conversion? Was it radical, more gradual, or somewhere in the middle? What was the key event, person, or thing God used to call you to relationship with Christ?**

- How might a person who feels that they have never really responded to Christ's invitation to live life with him?

- Have the sacraments of the Eucharist and Reconciliation helped you to mature as a disciple of Christ? If so, how?

> "God must give man a new heart"
>
> **CCC, 1432, Ezek 36:26-27**

Please invite a participant to read the following paragraph aloud.

If, like the prodigal son, you ever feel you have left your Father's house, the graces of the Sacrament of Reconciliation (also referred to as the Sacrament of Conversion) wipe away every mortal and venial sin. The grace received in the Sacrament of Reconciliation restores us to God's grace and joins us with him in an intimate friendship (*CCC* 1468).

When like the elder son, we recognize the need for ongoing conversion, frequent recourse to the Sacrament of Reconciliation is for the faithful what physical training is for champion athletes – a primary source of strength

> "The beginning of good works is the confession of evil works."
>
> **St. Augustine**

and excellence. As stated in the *Catechism*:

1458 Without being strictly necessary, confession of everyday faults (venial sins) is nevertheless strongly recommended by the Church. Indeed the regular confession of our venial sins helps us form our conscience, fight against evil tendencies, let ourselves be healed by Christ and progress in the life of the Spirit. By receiving more frequently through this sacrament the gift of the Father's mercy, we are spurred to be merciful as he is merciful.

At confession, telling the priest a little about your personal situation will help him lead you through the sacrament and set you at ease.

Connecting to Christ This Week

Christians throughout the centuries have done a nightly Examination of Conscience before going to bed. Take five minutes before bed each night this week to examine your day for God's presence and for the times when you sinned throughout the day. Thank Jesus for his love for you and ask his forgiveness for the sins of your day.

> *"Jesus calls to conversion. . . 'The time is fulfilled, and the kingdom of God is at hand; repent and believe in the gospel."*
>
> **CCC, 1427; Mk 1:15**

Take time to write down aspects from your past that make it hard to see the depth of the Father's love for you. Making those things known to God can be helpful in beginning the processes of conversion. Ask for conversion and take time to wait on God and know him in his healing presence.

Reflect on your own faith story. Take time to thank God for the key events, people, books, etc. that he used in your life to communicate the depth of his love to you.

Often the Sunday Readings are listed in your parish's bulletin. You can also find them on-line at www.usccb.org/nab/. Take time this week to read through the readings and meditate on the verses that hit you personally. Thank God for the insights that you received and inspirations to commit yourself more fully to Christ.

Take advantage of the opportunity to be restored to intimate friendship with God through the Sacrament of Reconciliation.

Closing Reflection & Prayer

Ask someone to open up the group in prayer. Spend time together thanking God for the ways he has drawn you to himself. Close with this prayer by St. Ignatius of Loyola (1491-1556).

Take, Lord, and receive all my liberty, my memory, my understanding, and my entire will,
all that I have and possess.
You have given all to me; to you, O Lord, now I return it;
all is yours, dispose of me wholly according to your Will.
Give me only your love and your grace, for this is enough for me.
Amen.

Conclusion

As mentioned in the Introduction, the *The Way* series was designed to be more than a Bible study. Our hope and purpose was to encourage an authentic encounter with Jesus Christ, the source and summit of our faith. As they were for the disciples so long ago on the road to Emmaus, we hope that your "hearts were burning" as you encountered Christ personally through word and sacrament, reflection and discussion, solitude and community. We especially hope this experience of "opening the Scriptures" has better prepared you to recognize Jesus more profoundly in the "breaking of the bread" at Holy Mass.

> *"No demand on our ministry is more urgent than the 'new evangelization' needed to satisfy the spiritual hunger of our times."*
>
> **Avery Cardinal Dulles**

For some, the last six weeks may have spurred a spiritual awakening of sorts. Your faith in Jesus Christ and your friendship with him may have deepened, strengthened, and taken on a richer, fuller context. Through the disciplines of prayer, Scripture reading, community, and the sacraments, you may have heightened those encounters with Christ which continually give your life "a new horizon and decisive direction"(Pope Benedict XVI, *Deus Caritas Est*). You may be experiencing more of the "abundant life" (Jn 10:10) that can only be found in friendship to Jesus Christ. We join you in praise for the work that He has done in your life.

For others, this might have been the first time you have intentionally focused on your relationship with God. Maybe this is the first time you have ever opened yourself to a deeply personal friendship with Jesus Christ. Perhaps this small group has helped you to overcome misconceptions or even fears about the spiritual life. For the first time you may have heard the voice of Jesus calling you to follow him, to be his disciple in every aspect of your daily life. You might have even experienced a radical change of heart, an initial conversion that gives an entirely new and beautiful vision to your life. What a glorious moment this is! We lift you up in praise and thanksgiving for the new life that God has given you in Christ.

Regardless of your experience through *The Way*, the journey is not over. No matter where we might be in our personal journey of faith, Jesus continues to walk alongside us every day, meeting us where we are yet calling us to a place we have not yet been. Not only as master but as a friend, Jesus calls us to "put out into the deep" (JPII), to embrace the mystery of a life spent knowing, loving, and serving him.

Just as in human friendships, our ongoing friendship with God requires time, attention, and prayerful reflection. We must continue to invest in the precious gift of faith we have been given in Jesus Christ. Through the *The Way*

> "'Duc in altum!' Put out into the deep!."
>
> **Pope John Paul II,**
> ***Novo Millennio Ineunte***

series, we hope that you have developed the fundamental "habits" of discipleship — daily prayer, Scripture reading, embracing the rich sacramental life, authentic Christian community, and openness to ongoing conversion — that will help you maintain and strengthen your relationship with the author and giver of life.

It is vital that you continue in the practice of these disciplines in order to grow more and more into the likeness of Jesus Christ our Lord. May the conclusion of this first *The Way* series propel you into a new springtime of growth through your ongoing commitment to faithfulness:

- **Make a personal commitment to spend time alone in prayer everyday. Just as Jesus so often did, break away from the noise and the busyness of daily life to find that solitary place to commune with the Father.**

- **Dedicate a portion of your devotional time to reading Scripture. You may wish to follow the daily readings offered by the Church (see www.usccb.org/nab/). You may also want to prayerfully discern** a book or section of the Bible that you feel God calling you to – maybe a Gospel, the Psalms, or the Pauline epistles. Regardless of your particular reading selection, many find it helpful to begin with Scripture, providing spiritual "fodder" for their time in prayer.

- Commit to finding (or perhaps even starting) a small Christian community where you can continue to grow with other faithful disciples of Christ. This can be a very beneficial aspect of our ongoing spiritual development. Meet weekly for prayer, Scripture reflection, and discussion. You may want to try group *lectio divina*, a practice enthusiastically encouraged by our Holy Father, Pope Benedict XVI.

- And most importantly, embrace Christ in the greatest gifts he has given us: his very self in the sacraments. In addition to Sunday liturgies, make time to attend daily Mass when possible – prayerfully receiving our Lord in the Holy Eucharist. Foster a deeper friendship with Christ by spending time with him through adoration of the Blessed Sacrament in your parish. Receive Christ's forgiveness, healing and transforming strength through the Sacrament of Reconciliation.

> *"The greatness of the incarnation and gratitude for the gift of the first proclamation of the Gospel in America are an invitation to respond readily to Christ with a more decisive personal conversion and a stimulus to ever more generous fidelity to the Gospel."*
>
> **Pope John Paul II,**
> ***Ecclesia in America***

You have received "good news" indeed! Jesus is not in the tomb, but is alive and well among us. Awakened by the presence of Emmanuel ("God-with-us"), we too are compelled to share our experience of the risen Lord with those we know and love – "The Lord has truly been raised!" (Lk 24:34). May your mouth speak out of the overflow of your heart, remade and set ablaze by the power of God. And may the world come to know him through your enduring connection to Jesus Christ.

Appendix

Appendix

Not meant to represent an exhaustive list, the following resources offer deep and powerful insights into the spiritual life and the art of connecting to Christ.

- *Introduction to the Devout Life*, St. Francis de Sales.

- *The Spiritual Exercises* of St. Ignatius of Loyola.

- *The Dialogue*, St. Catherine of Sienna: Includes a treatise on prayer.

- *The Imitation of Christ*, Thomas A. Kempis. Widely understood as the most read text in the Western Church over the last 500 years (other than the Bible).

- *Interior Castle*, St. Teresa of Avila

- *Story of a Soul*, St. Thérèse of Lisieux.

- *The Practice of the Presence of God*, Br. Lawrence.

- *The Confessions of St. Augustine.*

- *The Cloud of Unknowing*, author unknown. A classic text on contemplative prayer.

- *The Ascent of Mt. Carmel*, St. John of the Cross. Contains his famous poem and exposition entitled "The Dark Night of the Soul".

- *The legacy of St. Francis of Assisi*, including the Little Flowers of St. Francis.

- *True Devotion to the Blessed Virgin Mary*, St. Louis de Montfort.

- *Revelations of Divine Love*, Juliana of Norwich.

- *Abandonment to Divine Providence*, Jean-Pierre de Caussade.

- *The Rule of St. Benedict*, see chapters 19 and 20 on reverence in prayer.

Small Group
Discussion Guidelines

Welcome to *The Way*, a small Christian community which seeks to foster a deeper and more meaningful connection with God and with one another. For many of you this will no doubt be a new experience. You may be wondering what will take place, will I fit in, and even will I want to come back? These are fair considerations. Here are some expectations and values to help clarify the character of this community. Please read the following aloud and discuss if necessary:

Purpose

We gather as Christians – our express purpose in gathering is to encourage one another in our mutual commitment to living the Gospel of Jesus Christ in and through the Church.

Priority

In order to reap the full fruits of this personal and communal journey of faith, we will make participation in the weekly gatherings a priority.

Participation

Each person has a unique relationship with God. We will strive to create an environment in which all are encouraged to share at their comfort level.

Discussion Guidelines

The heart of our gathering time is our sharing in "Spirit-filled" discussion. This type of dialogue occurs when the presence of the Holy Spirit is welcomed and encouraged by the nature and tenor of the discussion. To engage in such a discussion, it is important that all participants observe the following guidelines:

- **Participants give constant attention to respect, humility, openness, and honesty in sharing.**

- **Participants share on their level of personal comfort.**

- **As silence is a vital part of the total process, participants are given time to reflect before sharing begins. Also, keep in mind that a period of comfortable silence often occurs between individual sharing.**

- Participants are enthusiastically encouraged to share while, at the same time to exercise care to permit others (especially the quieter members) an opportunity to speak. Each participant should aim to maintain a balance between participating joyfully and no one should dominate the conversation.

- Participants are to respect with confidentiality anything of a personal nature that may have been shared in the group.

- Perhaps most importantly, participants should seek to cultivate a mindfulness of the Holy Spirit's desire to be present in the time spent together.

Time

It is important that your group starts and ends on time. Generally a group meets for about 90 minutes with an additional 30 minutes or so for refreshments. Agree on these times as a group and work to honor them.

Your Role as a Facilitator

Perhaps no skill is more important to the success of your small group than the ability to facilitate a discussion according to the movement of the Holy Spirit. Such an approach recognizes the prominence of God's sanctifying Spirit in the spiritual journey, not necessarily our knowledge or theological acumen. The following guidelines can help facilitators avoid some of the common pitfalls of small group discussion, and open the door for the Spirit to take the lead in the "connection" we seek with Jesus Christ.

You are a Facilitator, *NOT* a Teacher

It can be incredibly tempting to answer every question as a facilitator. You may have excellent answers and be excited about sharing them with your brothers and sisters in Christ. A more Socratic method however, by which you attempt to draw answers from participants, is much more fruitful in the long run. Get in the habit of reflecting participants' questions to the whole group before offering your own input. It is not necessary for you as a facilitator to immediately enter into the discussion or offer a magisterial answer. Matter of fact, when others have sufficiently addressed an issue, try to exercise restraint in your comments. Simply affirm what has been said, thank them, and move on. If you don't know the answer to a given question, have a participant look it up in the *Catechism of the Catholic Church* and read it aloud to the group. If you cannot find an answer, ask someone to research the question and bring their discoveries to the next session. Finally, never feel embarrassed to say, "I don't know." Simply acknowledge the quality of the question and offer to follow up with that person after some digging. Remember, you are a facilitator, not a teacher.

Affirm and Encourage

We are more likely to repeat a behavior when it is openly encouraged. If you want to encourage more active participation and sharing, give positive affirmation to group members' responses. This is especially important if people are sharing from their heart. A simple "thank you for sharing that" can go a long way in encouraging further discussion in your small group. If someone has offered a theologically questionable response, don't be nervous or combative. Wait until others have offered their input. It is very likely that someone will offer a more helpful response, after which you can affirm them by saying something like, "That is the typical Christian perspective on that topic. Thank you." If no acceptable response is given, and you know the answer, exercise great care and respect in your comments so as not to appear smug or self-righteous. You might begin with something like, "Those are all interesting perspectives. What the Church has said about this is. . ."

Avoid Unhelpful Tangents

There is nothing that can derail a Spirit-filled discussion more quickly than digressing into unnecessary tangents. Try to keep the session on track. If the group gets off on a tangent, ask yourself, "Is this a Spirit-guided tangent?" If not, bring the group back by asking a question that steers conversation back to center. You may even kindly suggest, "Have we gotten a little off topic?" Most participants will respond positively and redirect according to your sensitive leading. That being said, some tangents may be worth pursuing if you sense the action of the Spirit. It may be exactly where God wants to steer the discussion. You'll find that taking risks can yield some beautiful results.

Fear NOT the Silence

Be okay with silence. Most people need a moment or two to muster up a response to a question. It is quite natural to need some time to formulate our thoughts and put them into words. Some may need a moment just to conjure up the courage to speak at all. Regardless of the reason, do not be afraid of a brief moment of silence after asking a question. Let everyone in the group know early on that silence is an integral part of normal discussion, and that they shouldn't worry or be uncomfortable when it happens. This applies to times of prayer as well. If no one shares or prays after a sufficient amount of time, just move on gracefully.

The Power of Hospitality

It is amazing how far a little hospitality can go. Everybody likes to be cared for and this is especially true in a small group whose purpose is to connect to Jesus Christ, our model for care, support, and compassion. Make a point to greet people personally when they first arrive. Ask them how their day was. Take some time to invest in the lives of your small group participants. Work at remembering each person's name. Help everyone feel comfortable and at home. Allow your small group to be an environment where authentic relationships take shape and blossom.

Encourage Participation

Help everyone to get involved, especially those who are naturally less vocal or outgoing. A good way to encourage participation initially is to always invite participants to read the selected readings aloud. Down the road, even after the majority of the group feels comfortable sharing, you'll still have some quieter members who may not always volunteer a response to a question but would be happy to read.

Meteorology?

Keep an eye on what we call the "Holy Spirit barometer." Is the discussion pleasing to the Holy Spirit? Is this conversation leading participants to a deeper personal connection to Jesus Christ? The intellectual aspects of our faith are certainly important to discuss, but conversation can sometimes degenerate into an unedifying showcase of intellect and ego. Discussion can sometimes take a negative turn and become a venue for gossip, complaining, or even slander. You can almost feel the Holy Spirit leave the room when this happens! If you are aware that this dynamic has taken over a particular discussion, take a moment to pray quietly in your heart, asking the Holy Spirit to help you bring it back around. This can often be achieved simply by moving on to the next question.

Pace

Generally, you want to pace the study to finish in the allotted time, but sometimes this may be impossible without sacrificing quality discussion. If you reach the end of your meeting and find you have only covered half the material, don't fret! This is often the result of lively Spirit-filled discussion and meaningful theological reflection. In this case you may want to take another meeting to cover the remainder of the material. If you only have a small portion left, you can ask participants to finish it on their own and come to the following meeting with any questions or insights they have. Even if you skip a section to end on time, make sure you leave adequate time for prayer and to review the "Connecting to Christ This Week" section. This is vital in helping participants integrate their discoveries from the group into their daily lives.

Joy

Remember that seeking the face of the Lord is a joyful process! There is nothing more fulfilling, more illuminating, and more beautiful than to foster a deep and enduring relationship with Jesus Christ. Embrace your participants and the entire spiritual journey with a spirit of joyful anticipation of what God wants to accomplish through your *The Way* small group.

These things I have spoken to you,
that my joy may be in you,
and that your joy may be full.

John 15:11

Materials to Have at Your Small Group

Several materials may be very helpful to have on hand while facilitating your Follow Jesus Series small group:

Bible

You and all members of the small group should bring a Bible to each session. It's a good idea to bring extras, if you can, for those who might forget. We recommend the *New American Bible*, the *Catholic Study Bible*, the *New Jerusalem Bible*, which has excellent footnotes, or *The Catholic Serendipity Bible*, which is not as scholarly, but contains good devotional material.

Catechism of the Catholic Church

Most sessions include reading selections from the *Catechism*, all of which are printed out in text for your convenience. You will still want to have at least one *Catechism* at hand for referencing when questions come up in discussion. You might encourage all of your participants to purchase one for their own collection, as it is an invaluable resource for private study and reflection.

A Theological Dictionary

We recommend Image Book's *The Pocket Catholic Dictionary* by John A. Hardon, S.J. It offers concise definitions for a panoply of Catholic terms. As you are preparing for your small group, you may decide to make other materials available for purchase, such as some of the classic writings of the Catholic tradition listed in the Appendix. We have found this to be a great way to get good books into the hands of eager people.

Made in the USA
San Bernardino, CA
29 June 2016